You Can Be Sanctified Wholly

The Christian Living Series

I. Christian Action
   Albert Truesdale, editor

II. Christian Home/Family Life
   G. Ray Reglin, editor

III. Churchmanship
   Richard Neiderhiser, editor

IV. Practical Issues
   Lee McCleery, editor

✷ V. Spiritual Life
   C. Neil Strait, editor

You Can Be Sanctified Wholly

by

Richard H. Neiderhiser

Beacon Hill Press of Kansas City
Kansas City, Missouri

Copyright 1988
by Beacon Hill Press of Kansas City

ISBN: 083-411-2175

Printed in the
United States of America

Cover Design: Paul Franitza

The *Manual* quotations are from the 1985 edition.

Unless otherwise indicated, all Scripture quotations are from *The Holy Bible, New International Version,* copyright © 1973, 1978, 1984 by the International Bible Society, and are used by permission.

Quotation marked NASB is from the *New American Standard Bible,* © The Lockman Foundation, 1960, 1962, 1963, 1968, 1971, 1972, 1973, 1975, 1977, and is used by permission.

KJV—King James Version.

10 9 8 7 6 5 4 3 2

Contents

Introduction	7
What Is Entire Sanctification?	9
Saved from Sin	11
Consecrated to God	14
The Cleansed Life	18
Power to Live and Serve	21
Hindrances to Holy Living	24
Helps to Holy Living	27
You Can Be Sanctified Wholly	32
Sanctification and Self-esteem	36

Introduction

You are a Christian! You remember a time in your past when you became consciously aware that:

1. Every human being apart from God's grace is a sinner. ("For all have sinned and fall short of the glory of God," Rom. 3:23.)

2. Christ's purpose in coming into the world was to save us from our sins. ("You are to give him the name Jesus, because he will save his people from their sins," Matt. 1:21; see also John 3:17.)

3. This salvation is a gift from God to you personally and to everyone who will believe in Christ. ("For God so loved the world that he gave his one and only Son, that whoever believes in him shall not perish but have eternal life," John 3:16.)

4. You have become a member of the family of God with all the privileges that accrue to salvation through Jesus Christ. ("To all who received him, to those who believed in his name, he gave the right to become children of God," John 1:12.)

If you have been attending the Church of the Nazarene, you probably have heard your pastor, a Sunday School teacher, or one of your friends in the church talk about *entire sanctification,* or *Christian perfection.*

Perhaps you have also heard it referred to as the *Wesleyan doctrine of entire sanctification or Christian perfection.* These are terms John Wesley used to identify the experience and life-style that our Lord Jesus Christ described as loving God with all of one's heart, soul, strength, and mind, and one's neighbor as oneself (Deut. 6:5; Lev. 19:18; and Luke 10:27; see Mark 12:30-31). If you have not heard of these terms, you undoubtedly have some questions concerning them. And if you have heard of them, perhaps some things about them remain unclear for you. The discussion that follows will attempt to help you understand the scriptural meaning of these terms and to lead you into a life-style of holy living that they describe.

Many books and articles have been written on entire sanctification or Christian perfection, dealing with their theological and devotional aspects. An extensive listing of such works has been done in *Holiness Works: A Bibliography,* compiled and edited by William Charles Miller (Kansas City: Nazarene Publishing House, 1986). It includes the holiness classics as well as recent writings by many authors of the Wesleyan persuasion.

What Is Entire Sanctification?

The *Manual of the Church of the Nazarene* states:

> We believe that entire sanctification is that act of God, subsequent to regeneration, by which believers are made free from original sin, or depravity, and brought into a state of entire devotement to God, and the holy obedience of love made perfect.
>
> It is wrought by the baptism with the Holy Spirit, and comprehends in one experience the cleansing of the heart from sin and the abiding, indwelling presence of the Holy Spirit, empowering the believer for life and service.
>
> Entire sanctification is provided by the blood of Jesus, is wrought instantaneously by faith, preceded by entire consecration; and to this work and state of grace the Holy Spirit bears witness *(article X).*

This is a basic theological tenet of the Church of the Nazarene and is crucial to its statement of faith. It is not only a doctrinal statement of the church but also the church's expectation in the life-style of its members.

The word *sanctify* means "to set apart for sacred purpose." Entire sanctification, then, would mean to be entirely set apart for sacred purpose. As the sanctuary of a church is set apart for sacred worship and is thus said to be *sanctified,* so also a person who is entirely set apart for sacred purposes is said to be *sanctified wholly*. It is only as a person is entirely set apart for sacred purposes that he may love God with all his heart, soul, mind, and strength. This is the person's own responsibility. The words *total consecration* are used to describe this act of responsibility on the part of the individual.

But entire sanctification is not only a decisive act of entire consecration by the individual but also a distinctive act of God by which He *cleanses* the life of the person who is entirely consecrated to sacred purposes. Further, God the Holy Spirit fills the consecrated life with His indwelling presence and with power for service.

Entire sanctification, then, involves: (1) the prerequisite of knowing the sins of the past are forgiven by Christ's atonement, and the old life of sinful thoughts and actions has been changed (converted) to the new life of following Christ's example of righteousness; (2) the conscious act of consecrating all of life to God and the Lordship of Christ; (3) the indwelling presence of the Holy Spirit, cleansing and permeating the totally consecrated life to God; and (4) the infilling power of the Holy Spirit, enabling the Christian to serve God with his whole heart, soul, mind, and strength. So let's take a closer look at these four areas that are involved in the life experience of entire sanctification or Christian perfection.

Saved from Sin

The opening paragraph of this booklet assumes that you are already a Christian. It cannot be assumed, however, that everyone who reads these pages is a Christian in the biblical sense. Just because a person lives in a Christian environment, or where the Judeo-Christian tradition is recognized as the predominant religion and influence upon legal and civil matters, does not necessarily make him a Christian.

Since the act and life-style of entire sanctification are dependent upon the prerequisite of the act and experience of the forgiveness of sins, and upon faith in Christ as Savior and Lord (known by such terms as *regeneration,* being *saved,* or *born again*), the starting point toward the assurance of the life of entire sanctification is to make certain that the saving grace of God through Christ is presently operable in your life. So let's take a few moments and trace those steps that lead to the *regenerated* life, from sin to salvation.

First, we must begin with the basic belief that the Bible is the inspired Word of God, that it contains everything necessary to bring anyone to faith in Jesus Christ. Do you believe this? You probably do or you would not be seeking to understand what it means to be sanctified wholly. If not, before you can proceed in your quest for holy living, you must take that leap of faith to accept the Bible as God's holy Word, which provides everything you need to know regarding who God is, who you are, and how the two of you can know and understand each other in a righteous and loving relationship in this life. Read Luke 24:44-47; 2 Tim. 3:15-17; and Heb. 11:6.

Second, you must believe that Jesus Christ is God's Son, whom He sent to earth to live as a human being in order that we as human beings would be able to know God and live righteous and holy lives. Read "Article II. *Jesus Christ,*" under "Articles of Faith," *Manual.* Read also the Scripture references listed at the conclusion of the article.

Third, you must recognize that all human beings "have sinned and fall short of the glory of God" (Rom. 3:23). Not one of us has ever lived who has not committed sin, except for Jesus Christ, of whom Holy Scripture says, "God made him who had no sin to be sin for us, so that in him we might become the righteousness of God" (2 Cor. 5:21). This recognition of sin must be understood to be personal—*I have sinned, and I fall short of the glory of God.*

Fourth, the only hope of redemption, the forgiveness of sins, is through Christ's atoning sacrifice—His death on the Cross. Rom. 3:24 completes the statement of verse 23: "All have sinned . . . [but] are justified freely by his grace through the redemption that came by Christ Jesus." This means that Christ died for your personal sins, that His blood (the permanent biblical means of atonement) was shed (spilled, let, drawn) for the remission of your sins.

Fifth, since the sacrifice of Christ has provided the remission of sins, it is your next step to appropriate God's forgiveness by faith in Jesus Christ (Ps. 130:4; Acts 5:31; 26:18). Since you have sinned, you must ask forgiveness.

Sixth, accept Christ as your personal Savior, thus becoming a member of the redeemed family of God (John 1:12).

Seventh, read God's Word, the Bible, as often as possible, but at least sometime during each day; and follow its principles, which lead you away from sin and into righteousness (Matt. 6:9-15; 1 John 1:7).

If you are not certain that Jesus Christ is your personal Savior, then before you can enjoy the blessings of the sanctified life, you need to follow the seven steps above and pray a prayer of faith for forgiveness and acceptance into the family of God. Wouldn't this be a good moment to make that prayer?

Consecrated to God

Now that you are sure of salvation, that Jesus Christ has saved you from your sins, you are ready to present yourself wholly to God.

The act of consecrating everything in life to God has something of a dual function. *First,* there is the surrender of one's personal will in total obedience to the will of God. This surrender involves a discarding of all those things that, if allowed to remain intact, would be barriers to holy living. At this point the consecration is a part of the human effort or investment in the whole action of the work of sanctification. God's effort or response is now engaged to purify the committed life by the cleansing blood of Christ. *Second,* the natural response from a grateful heart would be to offer the cleansed life, now under God's control, as an instrument of righteousness to the glory of God and the ministry of His kingdom throughout the world.

The apostle Paul describes this consecration in Rom. 12:1-2. "I urge you, brothers, in view of God's mercy, to offer your bodies as living sacrifices, holy and pleasing to God—this is your spiritual act of worship. Do not conform any longer to the pattern of this world, but be transformed by the renewing of your mind.

Then you will be able to test and approve what God's will is—his good, pleasing and perfect will."

Here Paul blueprints the structure for the total consecration of life to God. With a sense of urgency he appeals to the Christian brothers to consecrate themselves as living sacrifices, holy and pleasing to God. Up to this point he has been writing about the doctrinal structure of justification* and sanctification. In chapter 5 he exposed the origin of sin and its infection of all humanity through the "one man," Adam, and the "provision of grace and . . . the gift of righteousness . . . through the one man, Jesus Christ" (v. 17). In chapter 6 he concluded that the Christian must not allow sin to govern him as an instrument of wickedness, but rather, to offer himself as an instrument of righteousness. The true Christian is set free from sin and has become a slave to God with the benefit leading to holy living, resulting in eternal life. In chapter 7 he discussed the internal struggle with sin. He described it as a war within "against the law of my *mind* and making me a prisoner of the law of sin . . . within my members" (v. 23). "What a wretched man I am! Who will rescue me from this body of death? Thanks be to God—through Jesus Christ our Lord!" (vv. 24-25). This led him into the

---

*The meaning of *justification* is easy to remember; it is "just as if I had not sinned." That is how God views us when we have asked the Lord Jesus Christ to forgive us for our sins and have been adopted into the family of God.

victory of chapter 8 in which he concluded, "Those who live according to the sinful nature have their *minds* set on what that nature desires; but those who live in accordance with the Spirit have their *minds* set on what the Spirit desires" (v. 5). In chapter 12 he picked up this matter that the *mind* is a gateway to living either the life of sinful desires or the life of holiness. And it is here that he urged the Roman Christians to be *"transformed by the renewing of [their minds]"* (v. 2, all italics added). It is also important to remember that in chapter 6, verse 6, Paul talks about "our old self" being crucified with Christ "so that the body of sin might be done away with ["be rendered powerless," margin; "destroyed," KJV], that we should no longer be slaves to sin."

He turns now to the applied use of these doctrines, which is the practical response of active faith. He wants to persuade his readers to consecrate themselves in such a way as to center life in the practical doctrine that has developed out of the mercies of God.

Complete consecration is also *your* next step in your quest to be sanctified wholly. Consecrating your life to God as a living sacrifice, sanctified (set apart) for the expression of holy living, calls for a renewed mind and a transformed life by His mercies. Conformity to the world should cause you to admit that you are the "change agent" (i.e., the one who directs change) under the influence of the sin nature yet resident in your life, thus bringing about the patterns of unholy living. And while the matter of *your personal will* is active in the consecration of your life to God (you are still the change agent), it is the *transformation* of your life by your now *renewed mind* that directs you in all you do. The body of sin having been destroyed by the power of the Holy Spirit and the cleansing blood of Christ, you are at liberty to give yourself unconditionally to God. Your cleansed life, certified as a living sacrifice (an offering set apart completely to God), is now a life opened to spiritual worship expressing God's "good, pleasing *and* perfect will," tested and approved in the real, everyday life situations. The cleansed life will be discussed in the next section, but the clear message here is that the "living sacrifice" presented to God is to be complete—nothing withheld. To be sanctified wholly means to be completely consecrated to God.

The Cleansed Life

The cleansed life is a part of the whole scope of entire sanctification. It would not be possible to consecrate a sin-oriented life to God with the expectation that He would bless and accept it for holy purposes. Sin, both the acts of sin and the sin principle or nature that causes the acts of sin, are out of character with His divine nature. Consequently, before all of life can be entirely consecrated to God, the sin principle or nature must be cleansed. When this cleansing takes place, the barriers to holy living are broken down. Nothing remains in the heart and mind that would purposefully estrange you from God. Your prayer would be like that of James Nicholson.

Lord Jesus, I long to be perfectly whole;
I want Thee forever to live in my soul.
Break down every idol, cast out every foe.
Now wash me and I shall be whiter than snow.

Lord Jesus, look down from Thy throne in the skies,
And help me to make a complete sacrifice.
I give up myself, and whatever I know.
Now wash me and I shall be whiter than snow.

Lord Jesus, for this I most humbly entreat.
I wait, blessed Lord, at Thy crucified feet.

*By faith, for my cleansing I see Thy blood flow.
Now wash me and I shall be whiter than snow.*

This grand hymn emphasizes the interdependence between cleansing and consecration. Holy living cannot be absent from divine cleansing and is dependent upon entire consecration to God. Rom. 6:18-19 clearly speaks to this: "Having been freed from sin, . . . present your members as slaves to righteousness, resulting in sanctification" (NASB).

The cleansed life has special qualities or properties about it. Some of the aspects of this grace of cleansing have already been discussed; most notably and foremost is the change in the inner self. Whereas the sin nature was in control, resulting in sinful acts, the cleansed child of God operates from a renewed inner self, resulting in holy living. The manner in which the cleansed person perceives his relationship to God and others operates not from a sinful bias but from the bias of holiness. The cleansed or sanctified person always asks this primary question in every aspect of life: "Am I attacking and responding to life within the freedom of the parameters God has established for holy living?"* The cleansed and con-

---

*The parameters within which holy living is developed have been established by our Lord Jesus Christ in Luke 10:27, taken from Deut. 6:5 and Lev. 19:18: " 'Love the Lord your God with all your heart and with all your soul and with all your strength and with all your mind'; and, 'Love your neighbor as yourself.' " See also Mark 12:30-31.

secrated person pursues this question relentlessly. It becomes as fundamental and essential as breathing is to life.

Cleansing is God's act through Christ's atonement by which in regeneration the acts of sin are forgiven and washed away, by which also in entire sanctification the sin principle or nature is destroyed, leaving the heart pure. *Consecration* is our act of presenting to God the life He has cleansed so that we should no longer serve the desires of the sinful nature but serve our holy God in perfect love with all our heart, soul, mind, and strength, and our neighbor as ourself.

Power to Live and Serve

The work of the indwelling presence of the Holy Spirit of God is not concluded with the consecration of a cleansed heart and life. When the cleansing power of the Holy Spirit is appropriated, there is also at once an accompanying power in the life of the believer. The Holy Spirit expressed His power when in Christ He brought us from sin to salvation. He engaged His power to cleanse us through Christ's atonement. The words of these past two sentences run by us with such rapidity that we scarcely take the time to appreciate the great demonstration of divine power they contain. God actually forgives our sins and takes away the guilt that accompanies them! He actually crushes (destroys) the sin principle within us in preparation for our covenant to be totally His forever! What a display of power! Who on earth has that kind of power? It cannot be matched or simulated.

Several scriptures speak directly to the power that accompanies entire sanctification. In Luke 24:49 Jesus said to His disciples, "I am going to send you what my Father has promised; but stay in the city until you have been clothed with power from on high." And again in Acts 1:8, just before Christ was taken up into heaven,

He told His disciples, "You will receive power when the Holy Spirit comes on you; and you will be my witnesses in Jerusalem, and in all Judea and Samaria, and to the ends of the earth." The Book of Acts continues with the exciting narrative in which this promise was fulfilled. Peter is a good example as to the effect of such an empowerment. Whereas he was unwilling to identify himself as a disciple of Christ when confronted with a young girl at the time of Christ's trial and crucifixion, now, filled with the Holy Spirit and power, he stands before a crowd on the Day of Pentecost and faces the rulers of Israel with the message of salvation through Jesus Christ. The power of the Holy Spirit enabled him to witness.

Since entire sanctification deals with every aspect of life, the gift and grace of power that the Holy Spirit bestows on the sanctified life deals also with every aspect of life. Power is given, not only for such boldness to testify and exhort as Peter demonstrated, but also for calmness in the frustration of life's storms, strength in time of weakness, stability when all else seems to crumble, and humility even when assertiveness is necessary.

The Holy Spirit gives us power *to be* the holy person He desires us to be. Without this indwelling power *to be,* attempts at holy living would be reduced to "having a form of godliness but denying its power" (2 Tim. 3:5). It is possible for many people to *do* religion within the scope of their own natural gifts and talents, to merely *perform* the acts of the holiness life-style. But there is no substitute for the authentic power for life and service that the Holy Spirit provides when He sanctifies you wholly.

Hindrances to Holy Living

The life of entire sanctification or holy living must be perceived as a life-style. It is not a set of rules and regulations by which one is judged holy, although there are standards of behavior and attitude (mind-set) that do identify and define the life-style of holy living.

There is a superb direction from Holy Scripture that establishes the principle by which holy living may be identified and defined. It is in 1 John 2:15-17. What makes it such a superb direction is that it harmonizes precisely with Christ's instruction (Luke 10:27) to love God with the whole of one's being. "Do not love the world or anything in the world. If anyone loves the world, the love of the Father is not in him. For everything in the world—the cravings of sinful man, the lust of his eyes and the boasting of what he has and does—comes not from the Father but from the world. The world and its desires pass away, but the man who does the will of God lives forever."

The Church of the Nazarene recognizes that there are many areas of life that attach to *worldliness*. The General Rules of the Church of the Nazarene (*Manual,* under Part II) and the Special Rules (Part III) list those areas of life that typify the sins of worldliness. The list is not intended to be exhaustive or exclusive of other worldly matters that would also hinder holy living, but is meant to contain examples of the kinds of things that would prevent holy living. In these examples the principles governing a holy life-style are clear and are given biblical reference. Anyone following the light of Holy Scripture and a personal covenant to love God with his whole being should be able to discern the principles behind these *Manual* admonitions and scrutinize and evaluate life to the exclusion of worldliness.

Hindrances to holy living or entire sanctification center around the free will that God has given to everyone. It is a matter of one's personal choice to align his will with the will of God, to bring all of life into harmony with God's will. Those matters that prevent one from aligning his will with the will of God are hindrances to holy living. Some of the things hindering the Holy Spirit-filled life of entire sanctification are *pride, selfishness, hypocrisy, jealousy, lust, dishonesty, the love of money and possessions, a thirst for worldly power, an unteachable spirit, a willingness to compromise with the world and sin, too great a sensitivity to praise or blame, fear of acknowledging Christ as Savior and Lord, not reading and searching out the principles of holy living in the Word of God, trying to hold on to some form or forms of worldliness,* and *a lack of trust in God.* The all-encompassing love of God ruling and reigning in one's heart and life cannot exist if such things are allowed to be in control. Only the cleansing, indwelling presence of the Holy Spirit can bring power and victory over such matters.

Helps to Holy Living

When we are sanctified wholly, we are not left to our own devices to eke out a holy existence. The abiding Holy Spirit, as Christ promised in John 14:15-27, is the Divine Enabler who is the Advocate and Counselor, who stands alongside the sanctified Christian, guiding, teaching, prompting, and supporting him in every moment of life.

While it is the Holy Spirit who brings power and victory for holy living, the sanctified person must cooperate in exercises of faith and piety. A part of Christ's prayer He taught His disciples in Matt. 6:9-13 reads, "And lead us not into temptation, but deliver us from the evil one." It is obvious that the Christian's dependence is centered in God—"lead us . . . deliver us." But the cooperation of the Christian is implied by virtue of the fact that he is asking God for guidance and deliverance.

How is it, then, that the sanctified Christian is aided in holy living? *First,* there is the meditation on the Word of God. Holy Scripture contains everything necessary by which to live a holy life. It is imperative that the principles and practices of the Bible be read and understood. This daily exercise of personal worship and devotion produces the knowledge supporting who God is, who man is, and how God and man can experience and enjoy the divine relationship resulting in holy living.

Second, quality time spent in prayer enables us as sanctified Christians to be sensitized to the direction of the Holy Spirit. It provides a vehicle for *entrance* into God's presence; for *adoration and praise;* to *confess* our dependence upon God, our shortcomings, and those things that by human weakness we have neglected to think or to do; to bring our *petitions* to Him, asking for guidance, direction, strength, and the healing of damaged emotions and frailties from which the sanctified Christian is not exempt; and *thanksgiving,* which is the natural response of loving God with all one's heart, soul, mind, and strength. A certain group of men have a special prayer time with their pastor every Sunday morning at seven o'clock. For the past seven or eight years they have used this as a model by which to pray—*entrance, adoration, confession, petition,* and *thanksgiving.* It gives purpose, motivation, and direction to the Christian discipline of prayer.

Third, dwell on the things of God. Your salvation from sin is a marvelous thing. It must never be taken for granted. It is only by the grace of God that you are saved and cleansed. It is only by the power of the indwelling presence of the Holy Spirit that you can live victoriously in this world. God has given you the right to belong to the family of God, with all the rights and privileges of a family member. With the Holy Spirit present in your life, your body is the temple of God, and you should care for it as a faithful steward, watching after its well-being, preserving it for use as an instrument of righteousness unto the Lord.

Fourth, the corporate worship of the church is a means of grace that must not be neglected or ignored. Many radio and television ministries are helpful to those who are temporarily prevented from attending worship services in a local church. Those who are ill or bedfast undoubtedly find a great deal of spiritual comfort in some of these ministries. Even at that, there is no substitute for the "godly care of pastors, with the teachings of the Word; and the helpful inspiration of social worship" (*Manual,* par. 801). There is also the fellowship with other Christians who share the same joys and concerns as you do. There is the singing of hymns and gospel songs that admonish and encourage, support and strengthen the Body of Christ (all Christians). There is the bonding of Christian love supporting and unifying the congregation. There is the witness to the keeping power of the grace of God, and the helpful assurance of God's protecting and providing care. There is also the ministry of laypersons as they do good to all people, expressing in word and deed the virtues and life-style of holy living.

Fifth, be sensitive to the Holy Spirit. Ask Him to help you be thoughtful regarding your relationships to God, your family, and others. Be aware of situations to which you may be able to respond just as Christ would respond if He were here in the flesh. In effect, be Christ for that situation.

A man afflicted with severe headaches was hospitalized for treatment. One day a fellow Christian stopped by to visit him. The visiting friend urged him to continue asking God for help and healing. "Oh," said the ill man, "I've been praying all morning long, and my prayers don't seem to rise from my bed. My head hurts so badly, I can scarcely think, I can hardly lift a prayer. I can't seem to reach Christ today."

The visitor responded, "Please, will you allow me to be Christ for you today? Take my hand. As you hold it, just believe that Christ is holding your hand. And as I pray to God, just believe that Christ is interceding with God for you." The visitor prayed, and in a few moments, with tears of gratitude, both men experienced the presence of Christ, and a restful endurance settled down upon the man afflicted with headaches. We can only be Christ for another if in fact we follow Christ's example of holy living.

Sixth, make it a practice to keep a journal of your spiritual journey with God. You will be surprised how much more clearly you will be able to identify those hindrances and helps to holy living that develop in your life. It will help you to be more objective as you view yourself in relationship to God and others. It will also provide a guide for your continued walk with God.

Seventh, share the story of your holiness life-style with a new Christian. As you lead another into this blessed experience with the Holy Spirit, your life of holy living will be affirmed and strengthened as He works through you.

You Can Be Sanctified Wholly

If you believe that Jesus Christ is God's Son, that He came into the world to save all who believe on Him from their sins, and that He is *your* personal Savior now, you are a candidate for entire sanctification. You can be sanctified wholly.

At the outset it seems like such a gigantic step of faith. That is true. Through our own resources such a wholeness would not be possible. In and of ourselves we cannot attain such a state of grace called entire sanctification. But our sanctification does not depend entirely upon our own efforts. It is the work of the Holy Spirit in us, requiring our cooperation in the submission of our will to His will in order that our lives may be under His full control. It is the emptying of ourselves only to be filled by His love and power by which we may live a holy life. The apostle Paul, in his first letter to the Thessalonian Christians, reminded them that such wholeness, such completeness, was provided by God. Catch the significant words that biblically validate this experience, making it possible and practical. "May God himself, the God of peace, sanctify you through and through. May your whole spirit, soul and body be kept blameless at the coming of our Lord

Jesus Christ. The one who calls you is faithful and he will do it" (5:23-24).

Follow these simple steps into the blessing of holy living.

1. As a Christian you have already taken the *first step* toward this second, definite work of grace called entire sanctification. It may be called *initial sanctification.*

2. The second step is to recognize that this is your own personal need. You remember earlier in our discussion we talked about the matter of the *acts of sin* and the *sin nature.* In your conversion your acts of sin were forgiven. Now you are asking God to take away the sin nature that is the direct cause of those sins you knowingly and willfully committed. This is the act of cleansing.

3. Having been cleansed by the power of the Holy Spirit in cooperation with the blood of Christ, you now want to take account of your cleansed life, offering it wholly, entirely to God as your act of consecration. This is a most significant step, for if anything is held back, your consecration will not be complete, and the Holy Spirit cannot finish His sanctifying work of grace in your heart and life.

4. Having made your consecration complete, you must recognize that the Holy Spirit needs to possess every aspect and breath of your life. The hymn of Thomas O. Chisholm expresses it well:

Oh, to be like Thee! blessed Redeemer,
  This is my constant longing and prayer.
Gladly I'll forfeit all of earth's treasures,
  Jesus, Thy perfect likeness to wear.

Oh, to be like Thee! While I am pleading,
  Pour out Thy Spirit, fill with Thy love.
Make me a temple meet for Thy dwelling;
  Fit me for life and heaven above.

Oh, to be like Thee! Oh, to be like Thee,
  Blessed Redeemer, pure as Thou art!
Come in Thy sweetness, come in Thy fullness;
  Stamp Thine own image deep on my heart.

Ask the Holy Spirit to take His residence in your heart and life, infusing you with the very image of our Lord Jesus Christ.

5. By faith, just as you accepted Christ as Savior, believe that the Holy Spirit now fills you with love and power to be and do all that is necessary for you to be the express image of Christ in this world. The Holy Spirit will enable you to live out the reputation of Christ. You will love the Lord your God with all your heart, soul, mind, and strength, and your neighbor as yourself. The power and presence of the Holy Spirit, whom Christ said He would send to aid you (John 14), will accomplish this in you.

6. Now give witness to the blessing of entire sanctification. Perhaps the last verse of the hymn "Whiter than Snow" will help you express what has happened in you.

The blessing [entire sanctification] by faith I
   receive from above.
Oh, glory! My soul is made perfect in love.
My prayer has prevailed, and this moment I know
The Blood is applied, I am whiter than snow.

Remember, while there is a great deal of human emotion attached to such a deliverance from the bondage of sin, entire sanctification is a work of grace performed in you by the Holy Spirit. Let your emotions express your inner self in the reverence of holy joy. And let your mind bear witness to this clear and definite transformation.

Find someone close to you with whom you can share this clear-cut experience of Christian perfection. Tell that person what has happened in your life. Don't worry whether or not you are giving everything the right terminology. Just tell your experience as it has happened to you. Give praise to God with thanksgiving for His faithfulness in bringing you into the blessing of holy living.

Sanctification and Self-esteem

Sanctified persons too often misunderstand what has happened in the work of the Holy Spirit when He cleanses them from the sin *nature.* Ross H. Minkler wrote a song that was well known in evangelical circles, the chorus of which begins, "Let me lose my life and find it, Lord, in Thee; / May all self be slain, my friends see only Thee."* The intent of the song is to convey the concept of the total surrender of all that one ever longed for to God and the purposes of His kingdom. This intent is correct. But the second line of this song can be misleading: "May all self be slain." Entire sanctification does not make you *selfless.* It makes a change, a transformation in everything that goes to make up who you are and how you approach life. The consecration of everything in life to God includes the *self.* The misunderstanding of this experience often arises at the point where the sanctified person has come to believe that humility and pious living means being absent of the *self.* This cannot be true because our Lord's injunction to love God with all we are and have, and our neighbor as ourself, relies upon the sanctified self to express the total integrity of the transformed life.

---

*© Copyright 1943 by Singspiration, Inc. All rights reserved.

In the experience of entire sanctification the Holy Spirit prepares us, self and all, for holy living. Instead of all our energies and skills being directed toward our own interests and for the purposes of our own desires, they are directed to perform within the parameters of God's holy will. This means that all I am and hope to be is governed by the principles and the character of God's will. It requires my sanctified self to carry out God's will for my life. All the freedom gained when the body of sin was destroyed (as the apostle Paul expressed it) is expressed through my liberated self as I rejoice to do God's will, and take great pleasure in finding ways to carry it out creatively and positively.

To do God's will as sanctified persons challenges us to elevate our self-esteem to its greatest potential. This is a continual process in which we consciously, carefully scrutinize all that goes to make up life. There may be times when the best expression of our self-esteem would be simply to maintain a nonargumentative, nonaggressive posture while trying to evaluate objectively what is going on. There may be occasions when Christlike assertiveness best responds to the situation. In either case our self-esteem need not be threatened because we are responding in the spirit of Christ as His agent of initiation, reconciliation, or restoration, whichever the case may be.

Some things that lower our self-esteem may have a wide range of diversity. Usually, however, they come under the heading of those things that are not truly *willful sins* against God or man that nonetheless bring us a sense of guilt and worthlessness. Such things might be *omissions* (things that we ought to have done that may or may not have been within our ability to do), *human frailties* (things like slowness of mind, forgetfulness, the inability to assimilate information, etc.), *misunderstandings* (lack of perceiving the intent of the information received), *poor judgment* (insufficient information by which to make an adequate and correct judgment), and any other areas that might be attributed to our ineffectiveness. While we would not want to cast such problem areas aside as being of no account in our witness as sanctified Christians, neither must we hold them in such regard as being sources for our defeat as holy people. In such matters for which God does not hold us accountable because of our humanness, neither must we hold ourselves so accountable as to jeopardize our self-worth and effectiveness as His holy witnesses.

If you struggle with low self-esteem, there is a positive reinforcement you need to take into account. And it's not just a matter of psyching yourself up with nonsensical hype. When Christ redeemed you and the Holy Spirit sanctified you, you were regarded as fit for eternal life in God's heaven. And in the words of the late, great Baptist itinerant revivalist Vance Havner, "God doesn't have any junkyards for His saints."* So lift yourself up. You are worth all God has done at Calvary through His Son Jesus Christ. That makes you *someone* in whom the divine claims of worth and value have been invested. You need not suffer the struggle of low self-esteem any longer. And you can stand tall in the grace of our Lord Jesus Christ regardless of how rich or poor you are, regardless of your social standing, and regardless of the opinions of others.

May God grant you the industry and peace of holy living . . .

. . . through Christ our Lord. AMEN!

---

*In a sermon preached at Cedar Lake, Ind., in the summer of 1962.